Jimi Hendrix

Terry Barber

ENTERTAINERS

Jimi Hendrix is published by
Grass Roots Press, a division of Literacy Services of Canada Ltd.

www.grassrootsbooks.net

ACKNOWLEDGEMENTS

We acknowledge the financial support of the
Government of Canada for our publishing activities.   Canada

Produced with the assistance of
the Government of Alberta through the
Alberta Multimedia Development Fund.   *Alberta*

Editor: Dr. Pat Campbell
Image research: Dr. Pat Campbell
Book design: Lara Minja

Library and Archives Canada Cataloguing in Publication

Barber, Terry, date, author
    Jimi Hendrix / Terry Barber.

(Entertainers)

ISBN 978-1-77153-105-4 (softcover)

    1. Readers for new literates. 2. Hendrix, Jimi. 3. Rock musicians—United States—Biography. 4. Biographies. I. Title.

PE1126.N43B3495 2017   428.6'2   C2017-904627-6

Printed in Canada

Contents

Jimi's guitar lies on his bed.

Jimi's Passion

Jimi's guitar never leaves his side.
Jimi even sleeps with his guitar. In
the morning, Jimi straps on his guitar.
The guitar stays by his side all day.
Jimi practises guitar all the time.
Jimi has found his love.

Jimi wears his guitar when he makes bacon and eggs.

Jimi plays with *Curtis Knight and the Squires* in 1965.

Jimi's Passion

Jimi wants to learn everything about playing guitar. Jimi spends four years on the road. He plays with the best guitarists. He listens to the best guitarists. Jimi learns their trade secrets. Will Jimi become the best guitar player of all time?

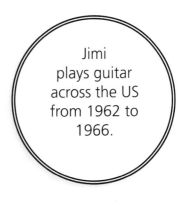

Jimi plays guitar across the US from 1962 to 1966.

Jimi uses his teeth to play the guitar.

Jimi's Passion

Many believe Jimi is the best guitar player of all time. Jimi can play a guitar with his teeth. Jimi can play a guitar behind his back. Jimi isn't a show-off. Jimi just loves to challenge himself with his guitar.

The Army uses this poster to
recruit men for World War II.

Early Years

Lucille and Al marry in 1942. Three days later, Al joins the Army. Lucille gives birth to Jimi a few months later. Lucille is only 17 years old. Times are tough. Black people can't find good jobs in Seattle.

Al leaves the Army and returns home in 1945.

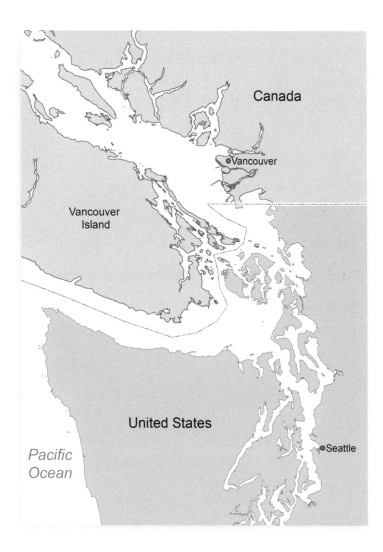

Jimi spends time in Seattle with his father and
in Vancouver with his grandmother.

Early Years

Al and Lucille have four more children. They like to drink. Their marriage is stormy. They divorce in 1951. Al raises Jimi in Seattle. Sometimes, Jimi is sent to Canada to live with his grandmother. Jimi misses his mother.

Jimi's father is Canadian.

A group of school boys.

Early Years

Jimi is a shy child. Jimi is also kind.
Jimi is funny. He makes others laugh.
People like Jimi. He meets all sorts
of people in school. Some are white.
Some are Asian. Some are black.
Jimi knows how to get along.

Jimi
likes to read
science fiction.

A boy places flowers on a grave.

Early Years

Jimi's mother dies when he is 15. Jimi is so sad. The loss changes Jimi. He feels like nothing really matters. Jimi fails Grade 9. Jimi begins to live every day as if it's his last. Planning for tomorrow isn't for Jimi.

In 1958, Jimi's mother dies from liver disease.

Jimi listens to all types of music on the radio.

Jimi's First Guitar

Music helps Jimi escape from the real world. Jimi likes to listen to music on the radio. He often strums a broom as he listens. Jimi gets his first guitar when he is 15. Jimi has no money for lessons.

Jimi learns by listening to others play guitar.

Jimi drops out of Grade 10 at Garfield High School.

Jimi's First Guitar

Jimi only thinks about his guitar. Jimi is never good in school. Now, his grades drop even more. In 1959, Jimi drops out of school. Bands are starting up all over Seattle. Jimi joins a band and plays his first **gig**.

Jimi's first guitar is an Ozark Supro.

Jimi's First Guitar

The band fires Jimi after his first **set**.
The other band members think he is
too wild on stage. Jimi *is* wild on stage.
He is also becoming a good player.
Soon, others want to play with Jimi.

A **paratrooper** drops from a plane.

Jimi's First Arrest

On May 2, 1961, Jimi takes a ride in a stolen car. The police arrest him. Jimi's lawyer works out a deal. Jimi can avoid jail by joining the US Army. Jimi trains as a paratrooper. After a year, Jimi leaves the Army. He has $400 to his name.

Jimi trains with the 101st Airborne Division.

Jimi gets a job backing the *Marvelettes*.

Jimi's First Break

Jimi makes a living playing guitar.
He travels across the US. Jimi plays
with many different bands. Jimi makes
little money. He is always hungry.
But he keeps learning. Then Jimi gets
a break in New York City.

Chas Chandler plays guitar with a band
called *The Animals*.

Jimi's First Break

In 1966, Chas Chandler discovers
Jimi. When Chas hears Jimi play, he
can't believe his ears. Chas thinks Jimi
is the best guitar player ever. But no
one knows Jimi. Chas takes Jimi to
England.

Chas is a
producer and a
guitar player.

Jimi arrives at the airport in London, England.

Jimi's Rapid Rise to Fame

Jimi arrives in England at the right time. England is home to rock and roll. Jimi becomes famous in no time. Other rock and roll stars love how Jimi plays. Jimi meets the Beatles. Jimi meets the Rolling Stones. Jimi is a star.

Jimi's band is called *The Jimi Hendrix Experience*.

Jimi is a rock star in England.

Jimi's Rapid Rise to Fame

Jimi's music flows from his fingertips. Jimi plays with no effort. People hear jazz in his music. People hear soul in his music. People hear rhythm and blues in his music. On stage, he is beautiful to watch.

Jimi's band tours Europe for two years.

Jimi wants people to hear and see his music.

Jimi's Rapid Rise to Fame

Music is more than sound to Jimi. The music scale has seven notes. There are seven colours in a rainbow. Jimi wants to play music in colour. He wants people to hear in colour. Jimi wants people to see his music.

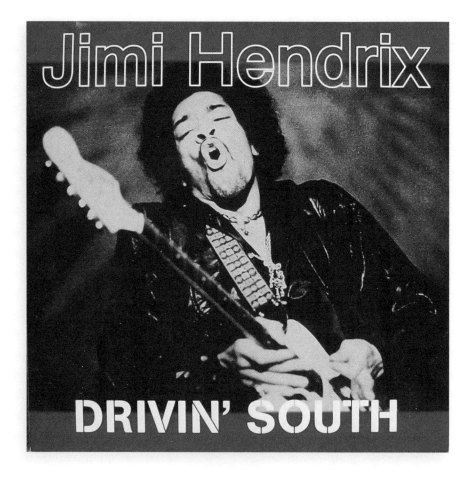

A Jimi Hendrix album cover.

Jimi's Rapid Rise to Fame

Jimi works all the time. He plays guitar. He writes songs. One of his best songs is called *Purple Haze*. The song's words come to him in a dream. The song makes Jimi a superstar.

Jimi writes the **lyrics** to 110 songs.

Jimi plays to a large crowd in the US in 1970.

Jimi's Rapid Rise to Fame

Jimi is a rock and roll legend. Rock and roll walks hand in hand with sex and drugs. Jimi returns home to the US. People line up to hear Jimi play guitar. Jimi is busy day and night. His health suffers.

People **protest** the Vietnam War.

Jimi's Rapid Rise to Fame

In the 1960s, the US is at war in Vietnam. Like many, Jimi is against the war. The **civil rights movement** also begins. People riot in the streets. When Jimi plays, people hear the cries of war and **injustice**.

Martin Luther King gives a speech.

Jimi's Rapid Rise to Fame

On April 4, 1968, Martin Luther King is shot and dies. Jimi plays in a club a few nights later. Jimi says this song "is for a friend of mine." Jimi plays for the soul of Martin Luther King. People are in tears. Jimi's guitar weeps with them.

Martin Luther King is a civil rights leader.

The memorial grave of Jimi Hendrix
in Renton, Washington.

A Sad Day

Jimi drinks some alcohol. Jimi takes some sleeping pills. The pills are stronger than he thinks. The mix of pills and alcohol causes his death. Jimi is only 27 years old. The world loses the best guitar player of all time.

Jimi dies on September 18, 1970.

Glossary

civil rights movement: a nonviolent protest
to gain civil rights for black people.

gig: a job for a musician.

injustice: a lack of fairness.

lyrics: the words of a song.

paratrooper: a soldier trained to land
in combat areas by parachuting from planes.

protest: to complain about something.

recruit: to encourage someone to join a group.

set: a group of songs that a musician or band performs.

Talking About the Book

What did you learn about Jimi Hendrix?

What words would you use to describe Jimi?

How do you think Jimi's childhood affected his life?

In what way is Jimi different from other guitar players?

Picture Credits